Vanito

J.S. Thomas

Copyright © 2013 J.S. Thomas

All rights reserved.

ISBN-13: 978-1490509082

DEDICATION

This book is dedicated to my nieces and nephews. Reach for the stars and focus on your dream of becoming who you want to be. Remember to keep Jesus first in your life and he will direct your path.

All rights reserved. No part of this book maybe reproduced or transmitted (by any means)electronically, mechanical or other means, now known or hereafter invented, including xerography, photocopying and recording, or in whole or in part, it is forbidden. Nor shall it be stored in any retrieval system.

Dream Big!

The characters, people, places, and names written in this book are fiction.

Share

Live

Dream

Smile!

Rejoice!

Imagine!

Forgive!

ACKNOWLEDGEMENTS

I would like to thank all readers who purchased this book.
May you find peace and happiness in your life.

Live

Vanito was a multi billionaire. He was very generous and caring. But one day a huge storm came along and damaged his home. In fact, he lost everything, including his corporation of twenty years.

But instead he didn't give up or become depressed. Yet he called his family and insurance company to start repairing the damages.

While tending to his home, he noticed a beach a far off. The waves were high. Tides began to flow. So, he stopped what he was doing to check things out. When he arrived, very few people noticed him in regular clothes. Basically, his usual suit and tie appearance was considered his basic attire whenever people saw him.

Well, Vanito thought of an idea. Why don't he observe the waves and tides to see if it is safe for people to be at the beach. So he sat at one of the concession stands. While waiting, he enjoyed a cool juice bar and ice cream sandwich. But still nothing was happening. Then, he got up from his seat and walked towards the souvenir shop. "Wow"! he said. "I never took the time to enjoy my life. I've been working and helping others, but not myself.

But as time went on. Vanito realized, while sitting, that he has no one to share his fortune or life with. Marriage was never on his agenda. Having children was out of the picture. So, he meditated and thought of an idea of dating. Yet he hesitated a bit. He thought "I want my wife to be special! Not just anybody. The person I want to spend my life with must be of good character. I refuse, he said, to be with anyone who just doesn't fit in my life style.

 I attend church regularly. But, just hanging on the street corners wasting time, is not for me. So, my wife to be must want something out of life. She must support and help our relationship. Hinder will not be tolerated. "I refuse, he thought, to be with someone who will tear me down. I rather be by myself, he said."
As time went on, he notices his watch. The time was 6:00 p.m. "I've been out at the beach since 12:00 p.m. That is the longest that I have spent enjoying myself. The waves and tides look OK! So, I better take a

couple of ice cream cones and head back to the house to finish what I started.

He arrived back at his home around 6:30 p.m. Stopping in his tracks caused fear in his mind. "Who been here, he thought." "How did this happen?" It looks as though, his house was completely repaired. Being mindful he ran to the front of the garage. He noticed over twenty people standing or just talking. One of them yelled, "He's here." Everyone shouted for joy. Vanito said, "What happened here?" "How did you all manage to pull this off? In the four hours I've been gone."

A lady from Davek Construction Company came towards Vanito. She said, "We assessed your damages days ago. We kind of planned to get you away from here by using the beach as an alibi. The waves and tides were created by professional boaters and surfers. So we figured you would, as always, go see about the people on the beach. Now, we manage to repair your home in that length of time. Basically, we started days ago and you just didn't notice. Today was the finish up day. So we had to get you out of the way."

"Well", said Vanito. "You all have done a magnificent job. Thank you so much. "One deed deserves another, said one guy. "Yes, you have been helping this city for over twenty years. You give to the homeless, created jobs, build homes for the needy, sponsor yearly Christmas dinner, help fund schools, issue $2,000 teacher bonus checks(

not tax deductible) to each educational staff of , serve on various committee and never ask for anything in return."

"Yes that's all true. But, I really want something in return. "I want a family to call my own. Children who will inherit this legacy. Great people like yourself to support me continuously. "Nothing in this life is more important than family. "I've spent all of my life with the Corporation of Vanito Switz. It has produced billions due to the software I created. But, I want rest now.

So Vanito got his wish. He married a lovely lady from Hopes town. They dated for a long time. He was able to have two children through their union.

But, Vanito didn't live to see his children grow up or graduate from college. He died two years later due to cancer. Lawyers of Hopran Law Firm gave "Mita" the wife of Vanito the LIVING WILL. The will stated he had $90 Billion Dollars saved to take care of his wife and children, $20 Billion donated to the school system, $100 Billion to distribute to all House of Worship within the city, $40 Billion to homeless shelters-children clubs, $10 Billion to sponsor Valentine –Easter- 4th of July-Christmas, and New Year Dinner Parties. Everyone would be invited, no exceptions.

In addition, a lifetime of funds was saved to continue Vanito legacies through his wife and children he called his own.

Even though the city suffered a loss of a

great person. But, they didn't loose his spirit. In his honor, the city declared a Vanito Holiday". "A Celebration of Life".

The End

www.ingramcontent.com/pod-product-compliance
Lightning Source LLC
Chambersburg PA
CBHW041618180526
45159CB00002BC/910